P9-AQZ-383

NOBODY'S PERFECT, CHARLIE BROWN

CHARLES M. SCHULZ

Selected Cartoons from
YOU CAN DO IT, CHARLIE BROWN Vol. I

A FAWCETT CREST BOOK
Fawcett Publications, Inc., Greenwich, Conn.
Member of American Book Publishers Council, Inc.

Other PEANUTS Books in Fawcett Crest Editions:

THE WONDERFUL WORLD OF PEANUTS	D1115
HEY, PEANUTS!	D1128
GOOD GRIEF, CHARLIE BROWN	D1129
FOR THE LOVE OF PEANUTS!	D1141
FUN WITH PEANUTS	D1133
HERE COMES CHARLIE BROWN!	D1113
HERE COMES SNOOPY	D1099
GOOD OL' SNOOPY	D1070
VERY FUNNY, CHARLIE BROWN	D1142
WHAT NEXT, CHARLIE BROWN?	D1140
WE'RE ON YOUR SIDE, CHARLIE BROWN	D1105
YOU ARE TOO MUCH, CHARLIE BROWN	D1134
YOU'RE A WINNER, CHARLIE BROWN	D1130
LET'S FACE IT, CHARLIE BROWN	D1096
WHO DO YOU THINK YOU ARE, CHARLIE BROWN?	D1097
YOU'RE MY HERO, CHARLIE BROWN	D1147
THIS IS YOUR LIFE, CHARLIE BROWN	D1164
SLIDE, CHARLIE BROWN! SLIDE!	D1197
ALL THIS AND SNOOPY, TOO	D1232

Only 50¢ Each—Wherever Paperbacks Are Sold

If your dealer is sold out, send only cover price plus 10¢ each for postage and handling to Crest Books, Fawcett Publications, Inc., Greenwich, Conn. 06830. Please order by number and title. If five or more books are ordered, there is no postage or handling charge. No Canadian orders. Catalog available on request.

NOBODY'S PERFECT, CHARLIE BROWN

This book, prepared especially for Fawcett Publications, Inc., comprises the first half of YOU CAN DO IT, CHARLIE BROWN, and is reprinted by arrangement with Holt, Rinehart and Winston, Inc.

Copyright © 1962, 1963 by United Feature Syndicate, Inc. All rights reserved, including the right to reproduce this book or portions thereof.

Third Fawcett Crest printing, September 1969

Published by Fawcett World Library
67 West 44th Street, New York, N. Y. 10036
Printed in the United States of America

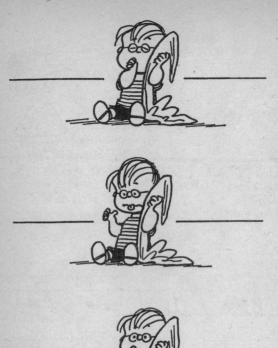

HOW HIGH ARE THE CLOUDS, LINUS?

OH, THEY'RE AT DIFFERENT HEIGHTS.. SOME OF THEM ARE "FAR-AWAY HIGH" AND SOME OF THEM ARE "RIGHT-UP-THERE HIGH"

WHAT SORT OF EXPLANATION IS THAT?

SOMETIMES IT'S BEST TO KEEP THESE THINGS IN THE LANGUAGE OF THE LAYMAN!

WHY COULDN'T MCCOVEY HAVE HIT THE BALL JUST THREE FEET HIGHER?

BOY, LOOK AT IT RAIN!

I'VE NEVER SEEN IT RAIN SO HARD FOR SUCH A LONG TIME..

I'M JUST GLAD I'M INSIDE..

WELL, GOOD GRIEF, ONLY A REAL BLOCKHEAD WOULD BE OUT IN A RAIN LIKE THIS...

WHERE IS EVERYBODY?

I HAVE A FRIEND WHO PLAYS THE ACCORDION..

HE CAN PLAY POLKAS, WALTZES, SCHOTTISHES...ALL SORTS OF THINGS..YOU KNOW, THE KIND OF TUNES THAT PEOPLE LIKE TO HEAR

AAUGH!

I KNEW THAT WOULD GET HIM!

SAY, THAT'S A BEAUTIFUL KITE, LUCY...AND YOU SAY YOU MADE IT YOURSELF?

IT'S VERY PRETTY...SORT OF A PALE BLUE, ISN'T IT? IT'S JUST ABOUT THE SAME COLOR AS MY.........

....BLANKET!

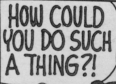

I NEED YOUR HELP, SNOOPY...

I WANT YOU TO START SCANNING THE SKIES...IF YOU SEE A LIGHT BLUE KITE, THAT'S MY BLANKET...

KEEP LOOKING UP...THAT'S THE WAY...LET ME KNOW THE MINUTE YOU SEE ANYTHING...

THIS IS RISKY...SOMEONE IS BOUND TO COME ALONG AND TICKLE ME UNDER THE CHIN!

LOOK AT THE LETTERS I'VE BEEN GETTING, CHARLIE BROWN..

HERE'S ONE FROM SOMEONE WHO SAW MY BLANKET FLYING OVER CANDLESTICK PARK IN SAN FRANCISCO, AND HERE'S ONE FROM OHIO, AND HERE'S ONE FROM MINNEAPOLIS...

HERE'S A PERSON WHO THOUGHT SHE SAW MY BLANKET FLYING OVER THE GRAND CANYON...

IT SOUNDS LIKE YOUR BLANKET IS REALLY GETTING AROUND

IT ALWAYS DID WANT TO TRAVEL..

OR WHY COULDN'T McCOVEY HAVE HIT THE BALL EVEN **TWO** FEET HIGHER?

WILL YOU BRING ME AN ICE-CREAM CONE, TOO, CHARLIE BROWN?

I WANT A CHOCOLATE-VANILLA CONE WITH THE CHOCOLATE ON TOP

WHAT DIFFERENCE DOES IT MAKE?

IT MAKES ALL THE DIFFERENCE IN THE WORLD... IF THE VANILLA IS ON THE BOTTOM, IT LEAVES A BETTER AFTER-TASTE!

LITTLE DID I KNOW THAT RIGHT WITHIN OUR OWN FAMILY WE'D HAVE A CONNOISSEUR OF ICE-CREAM CONES!

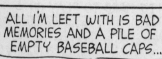

LOOK, SALLY, YOU'RE GOING TO HAVE TO GO TO SCHOOL SO YOU MIGHT AS WELL GET USED TO THE IDEA!

I GUESS YOU'RE RIGHT... I'LL JUST HAVE TO MAKE THE BEST OF IT..

I'LL GO TO KINDERGARTEN, AND I'LL STUDY, AND I'LL PLAY ALL THEIR GAMES, AND I'LL TRY TO GET ALONG WITH EVERYBODY...

BUT I WON'T LEARN LATIN!!

STOP GRINNING AT ME!

YOU SAY MY BEING A SLOW READER IS NOT CAUSED BY NEEDING GLASSES?

PROBABLY NOT...

SLOW READING IN CHILDREN IS OFTEN THE RESULT OF "MIXED BRAIN DOMINANCE"...A PERSON IS RIGHT-HANDED BECAUSE THE LEFT SIDE OF HIS BRAIN IS DOMINANT...

NOW, IF YOU ARE AMBIDEXTROUS, OR IF YOU HAVE BEEN FORCED TO WRITE WITH THE WRONG HAND, THIS MAY PRODUCE "MIXED BRAIN DOMINANCE"...

IF THIS IS TRUE, WE CAN RULE OUT POOR VISION AS THE CAUSE OF YOUR SLOW READING..

HAVE YOU RULED OUT STUPIDITY?

DO YOU PARTICIPATE MUCH IN KINDERGARTEN, SALLY?

I TRY NOT TO...I'M SORT OF HOLDING BACK...

FOR INSTANCE, YESTERDAY THE TEACHER WANTED ALL OF US TO GO TO THE CHALK BOARD AND DRAW, BUT I GOT OUT OF IT...

I TOLD HER IT WAS HARD FOR ME BECAUSE OF MY BURSITIS!

I GOT AN "A" ON MY REPORT CARD!

LOOK, I GOT AN "A"....SEE? RIGHT THERE! I GOT AN "A"!

YOU DIDN'T GET AN "A"... THAT'S THE PRINCIPAL'S MIDDLE INITIAL!

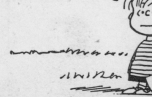

RATS! I THOUGHT I GOT AN "A"!

DEAR GREAT PUMPKIN, I AM LOOKING FORWARD TO YOUR ARRIVAL ON HALLOWEEN NIGHT.

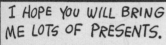

I HOPE YOU WILL BRING ME LOTS OF PRESENTS.

EVERYONE TELLS ME YOU ARE A FAKE, BUT I BELIEVE IN YOU.

SINCERELY,
LINUS VAN PELT

P.S. IF YOU REALLY ARE A FAKE, DON'T TELL ME. I DON'T WANT TO KNOW.

I'VE BEEN THINKING...

WHY COULDN'T I RUN OFF A FORM LETTER ON A STENCIL, AND SEND THE SAME LETTER TO THE "GREAT PUMPKIN" SANTA CLAUS AND THE EASTER BUNNY?

I DON'T THINK THEY'D EVER KNOW THE DIFFERENCE.... I'M **SURE** THE "GREAT PUMPKIN" WOULDN'T... HE'S VERY NAÏVE...

I WISH YOU HADN'T TOLD ME THAT... I'M DISILLUSIONED...

YOU MEAN YOU'RE GOING TO SEND THE SAME FORM LETTER TO THE "GREAT PUMPKIN," SANTA CLAUS AND THE EASTER BUNNY?

WHY NOT? THOSE GUYS GET SO MUCH MAIL THEY CAN'T POSSIBLY TELL THE DIFFERENCE...

I BET THEY DON'T EVEN READ THE LETTERS THEMSELVES! HOW COULD THEY?!

THE TROUBLE WITH YOU, CHARLIE BROWN, IS YOU DON'T UNDERSTAND HOW THESE BIG ORGANIZATIONS WORK!

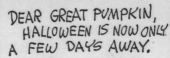

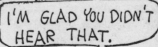

AND ON HALLOWEEN NIGHT THE "GREAT PUMPKIN" RISES OUT OF THE PUMPKIN PATCH...

THEN HE FLIES THROUGH THE AIR TO BRING TOYS TO ALL THE GOOD LITTLE CHILDREN EVERYWHERE!

THAT'S A GOOD STORY...

I PLACE IT JUST A LITTLE BELOW THE ONE ABOUT THE FLYING REINDEER!

ALL RIGHT, SALLY...YOU WANT PROOF...YOU'RE GOING TO GET IT...

WE'LL JUST SIT HERE IN THIS PUMPKIN PATCH, AND YOU'LL SEE THE "GREAT PUMPKIN" WITH YOUR OWN EYES!

IF YOU TRY TO HOLD MY HAND, I'LL SLUG YOU!!

I WAS ROBBED!

I SPENT THE WHOLE NIGHT WAITING FOR THE "GREAT PUMPKIN" WHEN I COULD HAVE BEEN OUT FOR "TRICKS OR TREATS"

YOU'VE HEARD ABOUT FURY AND A WOMAN SCORNED, HAVEN'T YOU?

YES, I GUESS I HAVE...

WELL, THAT'S NOTHING COMPARED TO THE FURY OF A WOMAN WHO HAS BEEN CHEATED OUT OF "TRICKS OR TREATS"!

STRIKE THREE!

THIS BAT IS NO GOOD! IT'S TOO LIGHT! THAT BALL THEY'RE USING IS NO GOOD EITHER!

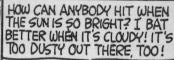

HOW CAN ANYBODY HIT WHEN THE SUN IS SO BRIGHT? I BAT BETTER WHEN IT'S CLOUDY! IT'S TOO DUSTY OUT THERE, TOO!

I CAN'T HIT WELL WHEN THE WIND IS BLOWING! THAT BAT I WAS USING IS TOO SHORT! IT'S HARD TO SEE THE BALL TODAY! YOU CAN'T HIT A BALL WHEN THE BAT IS TOO THIN! I THINK THEIR PITCHER IS..

GOOD GRIEF!

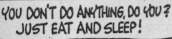

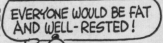

HERE'S SOMETHING I THINK ABOUT QUITE OFTEN..

I'M SITTING IN THE STANDS AT THE BALL GAME, SEE ..SUDDENLY A LINE DRIVE IS HIT MY WAY. EVERYBODY DUCKS, BUT I STICK UP MY HAND, AND MAKE A GREAT CATCH!

THE MANAGER OF THE HOME TEAM SEES ME AND YELLS, "SIGN THAT KID UP!"

HAVE YOU EVER HEARD OF ANYONE ELSE HAVING THAT DREAM?

ONLY ABOUT THIRTY BILLION OTHER KIDS!

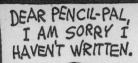

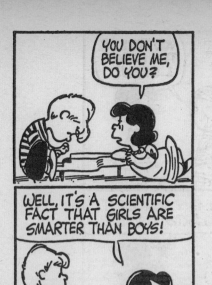

MISS OTHMAR IS RETIRING FROM TEACHING...

SHE SAID IT'S ABOUT TIME SHE STARTED TO RAISE A FAMILY OF HER OWN...

I ASKED HER IF SHE CONSIDERED THIS A STEP FORWARD OR A STEP BACKWARD, BUT JUST THEN THE BELL RANG, AND I NEVER GOT AN ANSWER

IT WOULD MAKE A GOOD TOPIC FOR A PANEL DISCUSSION